BMX
FREESTYLE

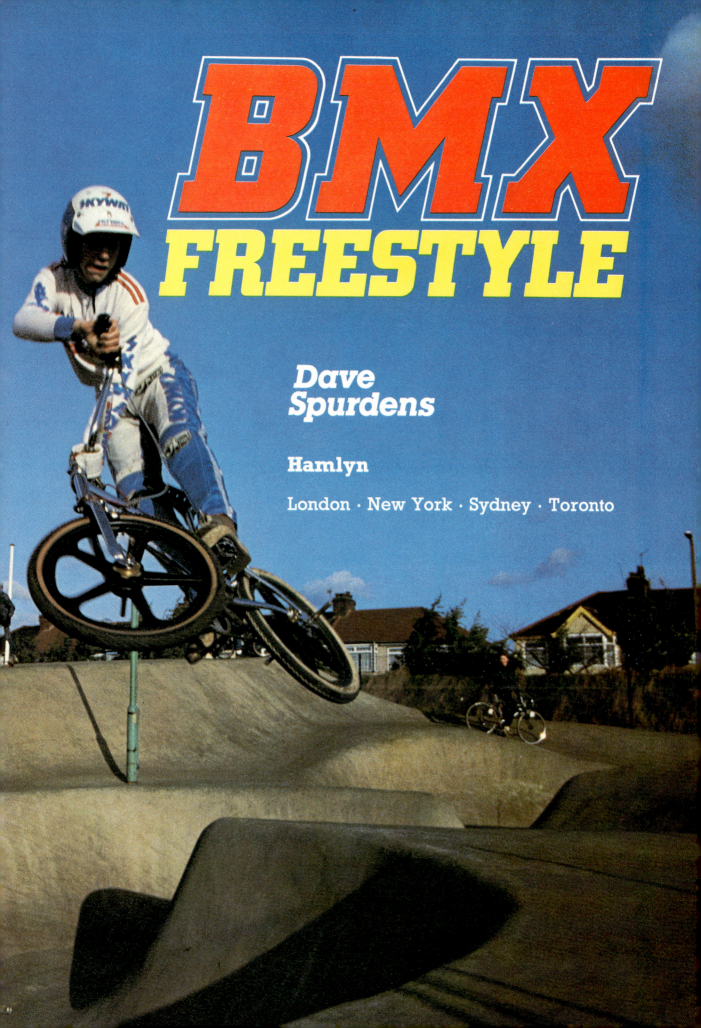

BMX
FREESTYLE

**Dave
Spurdens**

Hamlyn

London · New York · Sydney · Toronto

First published 1984 by
The Hamlyn Publishing Group
Limited
Astronaut House, Hounslow
Road, Feltham, Middlesex

© The Hamlyn Publishing Group
Limited 1984

Second impression 1984

ISBN 0 600 34775 3

Printed in Italy

All photographs supplied by
David Spurdens.

Contents

BMX Freestyling

There are two different aspects of BMX – racing and freestyling. Of the two racing is the more widely practised and more organized in the competitive sense. Despite this there are few meetings in the racing world where you will not see a wide variety of stunts being performed between motos (heats) and after all the excitement of the main competition has passed. For most riders the temptation of wheelieing or bunny-hopping is irresistible, and for those who gain a high degree of mastery over the tricks there are the serious Freestyle competitions where trophies can be won and reputations forged.

Climbing to the ozone. This rider has really got free of the quarter-pipe.

This is a famous racer but his freestyle expertise has helped him become the complete rider.

Some of the biggest names in BMX racing have also made their names as great stunt riders. Since BMX first began, a very wide range of tricks have been developed on a variety of different surfaces, varying from ground movements to short and long ramps. No matter where they are performed they all go towards making a more complete rider and establishing that much-sought-after 'oneness' between rider and bike.

In many ways freestyling has played a bigger part than racing in bringing the wonderful world of BMX to the notice of a wide public and certainly to the media. The spectacular leaps and incredibly ingenious manoeuvres have immediate appeal and a strong visual impact.

Freestyling has a further appeal to the BMX bike owner – it can be performed independently of anybody else. To race under rules with good competition, the rider has to depend on a lot of outside support, either from parents, sponsors or friends, in supplying the transport to meets, and the organizers who make the events possible. Not so in freestyling. All you need is a piece of waste ground and you are in business; and if you are a dab hand with the hammer and nails then you are really reaching for the sky.

Taking it right to the edge.

The important thing to remember about learning stunts is patience. To do it with safety the rider must make steady progressions and persevere with each trick until it is right. It takes a lot of work, but in the end the satisfaction it gives makes it all worth while. Before you start, though, read this book carefully. It is designed to take you along the right paths by giving you the right information on equipment, props and step-by-step breakdowns of the world's most exciting stunts. Remember – don't try anything flashy until you've mastered the basic techniques, and always wear the right gear. Have fun, but take care; that way you'll keep yourself and your bike together and in one piece for a long time to come!

Right: The trick may be finished but how you ride off the ramp is still important.

Below right: Putting the style into freestyle.

The Freestyle Bike

In the world of specialist stunt-riding the ideal bike is very different from the one you will see hurtling round a BMX track at a club or national event. That isn't to say that the bike you use on the track cannot be used for performing stunts. What takes place at the track whenever there is a spare moment belies that idea. What it does mean is that the racer will have to be selective about the type of stunt undertaken with a racing machine. Most ground stunts are within the province of a racer providing they are not tried on the real 'skinnies'. On the other hand some of the more hair-raising aerials might not do a great deal for the geometry of the racing bike. Having said that, I have seen riders on very lightweight machines performing very wild 360s over table-tops without sustaining any noticeable damage to their bikes.

Obviously a bike with specialist stunt equipment and construction is going to make life easier and increase the range of stunts attempted, and it is going to last a lot longer than the non-specialist machine. The problem with using your racer for sustained stunt work is that the damage is not necessarily evident until it is too late. The process of fatigue will take place

You need the right tyres when you are working on a high quarter-pipe.

When you are coming down from this height you need to get your landings right, even with a genuine freestyle bike.

This bike is suitable for freestyling but it is basically a racing bike.

over a long period of time and will suddenly manifest itself in a crack. One top rider, who had been doing demonstration stunt-work on two of his bikes, had both frames crack at the same race meeting. Another thing worth remembering is that no manufacturer will support his guarantee if damage is done to a racer during stunting.

So what is the difference between a good-class racer and a good-class stunt bike? Firstly the difference is in the frame. Whereas a racing frame will be made of 18-gauge chrome-moly tubing the stunt bike will have the thicker 16-gauge tubing, which is not only stronger but is heavier. On top of this it will have much sturdier gussets, welds and drop-outs. This all makes it too heavy to be a perfect race machine but it can, once the rider has grown used to it, be raced successfully.

The other major difference between the track machine and the stunt bike is the use of a coaster brake. This is a brake which goes into the hub of the wheel and is activated by the pedals. It gives the freewheeler greater control over his movement and is especially useful for giving that extra edge needed for ground stunts. It does however take a lot of getting used to, and only after a few months of patient experiment will the rider be able to use it properly. Once again, you can still freestyle successfully without a coaster, but you will do it better if you have one. Unfortunately, buying a coaster brake and mag wheels won't give you much change out of £60. Coasters can be put into existing wheels but it is a difficult exercise unless they are the plastic mag type.

There are frames which do however qualify as dual racer/freewheeler machines by virtue of their construction. The P.K. Ripper is one because it is heavily gusseted, as are the Torker and the Quadangle. The Quadangle is notable for its double cross-bar.

One factor that has a lot to do with the life of a stunt bike is the expertise of its rider in making his landings. This is why it is important to work up gradually to the more difficult stunts and ambitious aerials. It is equally important to have a tough pair of wheels.

Tyres are very much a matter of individual preference, though one or two factors should influence the rider's choice. The first is the surface on which the stunts are going to be performed. If it is quarter-pipe work with a very smooth surface then the tyre does not need the sort of traction required on the rough surface of a race track. The same applies to skate bowls and paved areas. Tyres with very close tread patterns are more likely to be successful on a smooth surface because more of the tyre is in contact with the surface. Where the ground is stony and bumpy then the tyre with well spaced tread patterns will grip some of the loose surface, and this is the type of tyre preferred by racers on the average track.

Lastly, the inflation of the tyre is very important, especially when the stunter is performing on a smooth surface. Remember the harder the tyre the less there is of it in contact with the ground.

Even though the real stunt bike will have a coaster brake it should still have two hand brakes. As you go higher up the ramps and further into the aerials the coaster brake can become more dangerous to use. When you make landings from height, the risk of the brake going on from an involuntary back pedal makes it wiser to use callipers and have the pedals in the forward motion position as you land. Whether to have one or two finger levers is a matter of personal preference. There are no practical advantages of one over the other.

Pedals take quite a thrashing in freestyle so it follows that the cranks are pretty important too. Here it is best to think basic. Any

good chrome-moly crank of the one-piece variety is suitable and will take the buffeting it is bound to get. Rather than the trick racing pedals on the market, the stunter should be looking for a really strong product. Rat-trap steel cage pedals are recommended, as are the very strong Shimano DX pedals.

Stunt-nuts are widely used by freestylers. These are extra-long nuts which protrude from the side of the forks and allow the rider to stand on them to perform various manoeuvres.

Bars and bar clamps are a matter of personal choice. There

aren't any bars, stems or clamps, designed specially for stunts, so check them out for strength and reliability, especially the clamp. The last thing you want when you're up there among the clouds is for your bars to start rotating.

Gearing is a matter of preference and age/strength ratios. Find the combination that suits you and suits the stunts you are doing.

Below: A freestyle bike – proper!

Bottom: A dual-purpose racing and freestyle bike.

Left: A bike with real freestyle wheels.

Below: Tyres are important, especially when you're on the top of the world.

These spokes will not relish the landing this bike is about to have.

Safety and Equipment

Make no mistake about it: freestyling can be dangerous and you can get injured. The most important thing is for the rider to be aware of the fact and take adequate precautions to minimize the risk.

In the first place wear all the protective clothing you would for racing. Helmet, gloves, elbow- and knee-pads and a mouth trap if your helmet is not fitted with a solid one. That's the rider kitted out, but there's just one thing – make sure everything fits you properly when you buy it, especially the helmet. It won't be very protective if it's dancing about on your head as you ride along. The smallest impact will have it off and then you'll be in trouble.

Personal protection is very important but so is the task of making sure your bike is safe. That means carrying out regular maintenance. The name of the game is making sure that a badly maintained bike is never the cause of you bailing out or sampling the soil. So check everything before you start freestyling. Below is a checksheet to get a bike in perfect running order before every session.

1. Make sure tyre pressures are right for the type of work you are going to do. Pressures will vary according to personal taste and for the surfaces.

This rider is taking a big risk working on a large ramp without wearing a helmet.

2. Brakes: check blocks for wear and positioning. Brakes are really important to the freestyler. Check adjustment and renew cables that have stretched. Check the callipers for central position.

3. Nuts and clamps: make sure they are all tight and that the handlebars and seat are positioned to your liking.

4. Chain: not too tight, but take up any slack.

5. Cranks, pedals and bottom brackets: if you've got a spider or three-piece crank then make sure all the Allen bolts are really secure, especially the central retaining bolt on a three-piece. Check for smooth and free movement, which you should have if you have been greasing the races regularly and cleaning away the grit. The same thing goes for pedals. Make sure they are secure and spinning freely.

6. Headset and handlebar stem: check for play. If you find it then you need to adjust them by slackening off the hexagon nut and tightening the knurled race with your hand, then re-tightening the hexagon. Check the stem bolt.

Remember, this is not a full maintenance chart. It is a pre-riding checklist which is the back-up to the maintenance you should have done earlier.

It's a good idea to get into the habit of doing your own maintenance, and checking the bike thoroughly after every major use. Get a BMX maintenance manual. Maintaining your bike means you'll know it inside-out, and it will be much less likely to fall to bits under you.

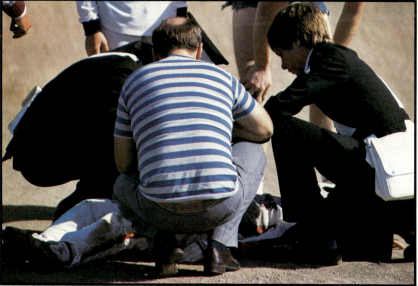

Top: This rider has the right gear on – good job he has!

Left: Luckily this doesn't happen often but it can be the outcome of a freestyle move when things go wrong.

Having gone over the mechanics there are still some very important things to be looked at. The first is to make sure you have all your pads and that they are done up properly. Never freestyle without pads, and a pad which isn't secured properly won't be a lot of help if it flies off at the crucial moment.

Next make sure your cables are secured to the frame and not flapping about in a wide arc from the bike. They're only little things but they can bring you to grief when you least expect it.

OK; you're dressed for the part, the bike's in perfect running order and the weather is suited to doing freestyle work. What next? Well, you have to make sure, if you are using a ramp or any sort of prop that it will withstand the treatment you are going to give it. The milk crate and running board is alright, but if they're not properly anchored to each other and to the ground then you could have serious problems. Much better if you construct a proper ramp and further on in the book we show you some easy ways of doing just that.

If you are practising ground stunts then you have to make sure that all elements of danger are minimized. Make sure you are well away from traffic and pedestrians. Try to select a surface which will give you a good chance of success. Clear the patch of any large rocks or obstacles and avoid ground which has a lot of trees on it, especially if you are working on fast ramp stunts. Particularly if you're using a ramp, always practise with a friend; then if one of you does come a cropper painfully, the other can get help.

Top: A helmet with a built-in mouthguard.

Right: A press-on mouth trap. Some riders prefer them for the better vision they afford.

20

Left: When you are working in a bowl, check that it is free of obstacles: bricks, cans or bottles can be a hazard.

Below left: Look out for people in bowls. Sometimes kids without bikes run around; and keep an eye open for the occasional skater – they're still about.

Below: Secure ramps. Make sure they are wedged or have rubber mats under them if the surface is at all slippery.

Ground Stunts

Every rider, from the time he gets his first BMX bike, starts the fascinating task of developing ground stunts. Probably the first experiment is with the bunny-hop over bricks or stones, and next comes the wheelie. These are the two most popular tricks and it is no coincidence that it is in these two exercises that world records exist.

The exciting thing about performing stunts on the flat is that you can always get to work without any equipment and set about making yourself a better performer. New stunts are constantly being thought up and anything you care to work out that is imaginative and skilful can be considered a stunt.

The bunny-hop

The bunny-hop is an integral part of freestyling but it is also a bona-fide racing technique which, once perfected, will make you a better racer. Bunny-hopping means to spring both wheels off the ground to clear obstacles. Speed is not an essential factor when you are approaching obstacles. Pedals should be parallel to the ground, weight over the seat and the body flexed low to the bike. At the moment of jumping the bike is pulled up. Once the obstacle is cleared the bike is let down, using the legs and arms to absorb the shock.

A joint pogo.

The wheelie

There are two popular types of wheelie. These are 'coaster' and the 'power'. The coaster wheelie, which is the more often used, is performed sitting down with the front wheel pulled so high that the centre of gravity is through or behind the rear wheel. Balance is maintained by using the back brake to prevent flipping over. For beginners it is useful to start on a hill.

For the power wheelie you maintain a strong forward movement to keep your balance.

Impressive ground work. A one-handed, one-legged hopback.

Rollback

You must master this one because it is the conclusion of so many stunts and it gives your tricks the sort of finish that makes them look smooth.

To start with, find a gradient and roll backwards down it. Before you go, though, make sure it's all clear. Stay in the seat.

The rollback is all about balance and it will help, even though you have a free-wheel, to pedal backwards.

The endo

The most popular endo is the 'kerb endo'. This is where the rider stops the front wheel against a kerb or low wall and brings the rear wheel as high into the air as he can. The back lift is achieved by shifting your weight over the rear of the seat and pressing down hard on the handlebars. The endo can be performed by using the front brake.

Endo with 360

Where a ramp is not available, this endo is best performed on rising ground. It needs to be a short slope because you have to start the endo near the top. Use the front brake to get the back high, pressing down on the handlebars, and with your main body weight to the rear of the seat. Shift your weight forward over the handlebars and, using your trunk, fling the rear of the bike round. Just before the rear wheel touches down, shift your weight to the rear again and roll back.

The racing spin-off for being good at endos is that if you ever endo over a table-top you are more likely to be able to cope with it, using this freestyle skill.

Pogo

The term, taken from the pogo stick, tells you exactly what you have to achieve. The idea is to get your bike up on the back wheel and bouncing about. To do this you need to use the rear brake. When you have it on, flex your whole body and pull up the front. Once you have the front wheel up extend your body and pull the whole bike off the ground. Keep repeating the exercise and you'll keep on pogoing!

Stunt-nuts are becoming increasingly popular and they are great for the pogo. The same principle applies. Apply the rear brake, stand on the stunt-nuts and, flexing and extending your body, start bouncing.

Endo: 1. *Ride the bike at medium pace with you weight just off the seat*

2. *Stand high on the pedals and shift body weight over the bars*

Pogo: 1. *Ride medium pace*

2. *Shift weight to rear of seat*

Buckin' Bronco: 1. *Get into the pogo position.*

2. *Shift weight over bars and push down*

3. *Apply front brake, push down on bars and shift body weight to back wheel*

4. *Hold it!*

3. *Pull up on bars*

4. *Flex body, pull up on bars and use whole body to bounce on the rear wheel.*

3. *Once forward position is achieved and you are bouncing on the front wheel, balance weight over the seat to stop you going over the bars*

4. *After several bounces on the front wheel transfer weight over back wheel and pull on bars to get back to the pogo position.*

Slalom riding

This is a manoeuvre rather than a stunt, but nevertheless forms an important part of being a good freestyler, especially if you fancy entering competitions.

Slaloms are great fun, whether you use them for a speed run or to see how smoothly and stylishly you can negotiate them. Most competitions judge them on style but it is possible to put them on the clock.

Balance is the all-important factor. Each rider has his own style but as a rule you should coast into the obstacles with your pedals parallel, and pedal between obstacles. Where the obstacles are really close it may be necessary to pedal continuously and regulate the pace by using the brakes.

Flat 180 flyout

This stunt is performed flying out of a graded rise, or out of the Bowl.

Roll at moderate speed, standing on your pedals. Flex your body and arms. Extend your body and arms, lifting the bike off the ground and slinging it round. Do not use the brakes. Finish off by rolling back out of it.

Flat 180 flyout with 180 pivot

The first part of this stunt is the same as the previous one but instead of rolling back the body is again flexed, the front wheel pulled up and the upper body used to spin the bike round balancing on the rear wheel. When the front wheel touches down, ride out.

360 off a short gradient

The run-up to this stunt needs to be fairly fast. Just before you reach the top of the gradient flex both body and arms. At the top, pull the bike up and using the upper body and arms heave the bike round until you land facing the way you were travelling in the first place.

Rollback and slider

Roll back down a good gradient until you are at maximum speed then stand on your pedals with your weight over the seat but leaning forward. Quickly turn the bars at right-angles to the frame, leaning the body to the side of the bike in the direction you are sliding.

Framestand

A spectacular one. It is easier if you have a double tube at the top of your frame but still possible if you haven't. Some sort of tape helps (but it's not essential) if you don't want to desacrate your beautiful frame. Get a nice even piece of ground with a reasonable run. When the bike is rolling smoothly hoist yourself up onto the frame using your arms. Achieve balance by holding the bars and getting a good position with your feet. Once you feel the balance is right, start to straighten up slowly until you get upright. Then just wait for the cheers.

The classic endo.

Great fun and it looks good.

Right: A pogo on the stunt-nuts with front wheel spinning.

Below: A wheelstand.

Bottom: Getting ready to pivot after a hopback.

Rockwalk

Rockwalking is really a series of pivots alternating the leading wheel. When you decide to make your first pivot, stand on the pedals and throw your weight forward over the bars lifting the back wheel just off the ground; then sling the back wheel round until you complete 180°. Now set your weight to the rear, pull up on the bars and spin the bike round for the next 180°.

Wheelstand

Turn your wheel at right-angles to the rest of the bike. Holding the bars get one foot on the tyre, followed by the other. You'll wobble a bit until you get the balance right. First let go with one hand and then the other to take up a straight balance on the tyre.

Astride ride

You need the stunt-nuts for this one. Get the bike rolling smoothly. With the pedals perpendicular, hook the left leg over the seat and onto the rear stunt-nut. Then shift the other foot to the front stunt-nut. Make a starshape for good effect.

Variations for the wheelie

One-hander Same technique as for the coaster wheelie, then let go of one bar and give a flash salute.
One-footer Same technique as for the coaster wheelie, then take one foot off the pedal and throw it out forwards and sideways.

Variations for the pogo

One hander As for the pogo but release one hand and hold aloft.
One footer As for the pogo but throw a leg out. If you have a coaster you can lift off the pedal pressing down to activate the coaster brake. If not you must lift off the pedal when it is perpendicular.

Wheelie: 1. *Ride seated, medium pace*

2. *Flex arms and lean into bike ready to uncoil*

180° jump off ground: 1. *Ride medium pace*

2. *Flex body in to bike*

Bar-hop: 1. *Ride medium pace, standing*

2. *Push weight forward and down on arms; bring feet off pedals*

3. *Pull on bars shifting weight to the rear of the bike*

4. *Keep the front wheel high by regulating your pace: too fast and you will come off at the back, too slow and the front wheel will drop.*

3. *Pull up on bars and straighten legs, flicking bike round as it lifts off the ground*

4. *Keep turning, keeping your legs and arms extended; land softly by flexing in to the bike again.*

Variation for the endo

Front foot clamp Same sequence as for the kerb endo or the front brake endo, but for this one the sudden stop is achieved by clamping a foot on the tyre underneath the fork arch. Practise this gently at first because it can be painful if you are going too fast or if you push the foot too far under the fork arch.

Bar hop

Roll along at medium pace. Rock to and fro on the seat and flex your body for the big lift. With arms straightened and gripping the bars, push down and bring your rear off the seat. At the same time bring your knees up into your body and clear the bars. Now let yourself down on the bars and sit there, steering with your backside and balancing with your whole body.

180 pogo spiral

As for the pogo but once you're up there and bouncing well, grip the bars and fling the bike round so you move in a circle.

3. *Tuck knees up into chest*

4. *Balancing on extended arms push feet over bars*

5. *Variation – No hands.*

Small Ramp

Moving from ground tricks to the small ramp is a step forward to becoming a complete stunter. You have to get used to the art of judging how far up the ramp you can go and the sensation of knowing there's nothing either side of you when you are up there. Make sure your ramp is secured and on level ground. To start with, just get used to rolling up the ramp and performing simple rollbacks. Once you're happy with your judgement you can take on the basic kickturn, but do it halfway down the board at first, just to get the feel of things. This is the key to ramp work, which can be dangerous if you don't know what you are doing. The secret is: progressive steps.

Endo, no feet and nearly O.T.T.

Above: A one-handed cross-up kickturn.

Above left: One-foot one-hand kickturn.

Great stuff at the end of a short ramp.

Rollback off a small ramp

Approach the ramp at medium speed, and get as high up it as you can without going over the top. Because of the difference in angles it is not necessary to stand on the pedals. When you get to the top apply both brakes and pull back on the bars. Keep your weight forward and pedal backwards to assist balance.

Kickturn

Make a medium-paced approach and, once you're on the ramp, stand with your weight above the pedals. The higher you get the more you shift your weight to the back. As you get to the lip lift the bars as you would for the start of a wheelie. Apply the back brake and pivot the bike round. Once you've turned 180° hold your weight back and let the front wheel down. Ride off the ramp. Aim to kick the rear wheel out sideways.

Hopback on the small ramp.

Approach the ramp at a medium pace. As you reach the top, shift your weight to the back and pull up on the bars, applying both brakes as you do so. Once you are up in the pogo position start jumping, keeping the back brake on, and pogo back down.

Hopback on a small ramp on stunt-nuts

Ride at medium pace to the ramp. At the bottom, transfer from pedals to stunt-nuts and coast up the ramp in this position. When you get to the top, pull up on the bars. When the front wheel is up, hop on the back wheel to the bottom.

Ramp endo and rollback

Approach the ramp at medium pace. At the ramp, stand on the pedals. As you near the top shift your weight forward and apply the front brake. When you push forward you should be in a standing position. From the moment you feel the back lifting, shift your rear over the back wheel but still push forward and

180° pivot: 1. *Ride up ramp medium pace*

2. *Apply front brake at the top of the ramp*

3. *Push weight forward and flick the back round, keeping the brake hard on.*

4. *Continue the pivot until the bike is straightened again.*

5. *Let the brake off and ride out.*

down with your arms. Keep the front brake on and slowly let the back wheel down. Once it touches the ramp, let the brake off and roll back, seated or standing.

Small ramp double jump

Into the thriller class now and you'll need all your 'bottle' to get out of this one! Basically you need two small ramps, spaced out but back-to-back. How far apart you have them is up to you. As usual when you're learning the ramps it's best to take it one step at a time. First of all have the ramps just a couple of metres apart and approach the first ramp at just above medium pace. Once you have take-off there are two things to worry about – are you high enough to clear the top lip of the second board, and do you have the right angle to make a smooth landing?

Right: A one-foot one-hand kickturn.

Left: A cross-up before riding out.

The first part is all about judgement, the second about skill. You'll get to know how much crank you need to give it to get the height and distance but to come in at the right angle you need good body control. Ideally, you want to be sailing through the air with the front wheel slightly up, and standing up with your weight over the pedals. At the point of touch-down, shift your weight over the back wheel, press with your arms to bring the front wheel down – and hey-presto, you ride out to thunderous applause. Well, you do when you get about ten metres between ramps!

Kickturn with cross-up

Same procedure as for the basic kickturn, with the difference that once you have lifted the front and turned the bike so it is at right-angles to the ramp, you cross the bars up until your arms are totally crossed and the wheel is turned right back. When the bike begins to drop you must uncross and get the wheel facing forwards, ready to ride out.

One-foot kickturn

Once again a variation on the basic kickturn. Again, things change when you get to the top of the ramp. At this point apply the rear brake, bring the front wheel up and start the pivot. If you have a coaster this trick is a lot easier. If you haven't then you really have to squeeze that rear brake while you balance on one pedal and kick the free leg out behind the bike. The leg should be fully extended by the time the bike has completed the 180°. Get the free foot back on the pedal, let the front down and ride out.

Right: Double-act on the short ramp.

Far right: Cross-up endo on the short ramp.

34

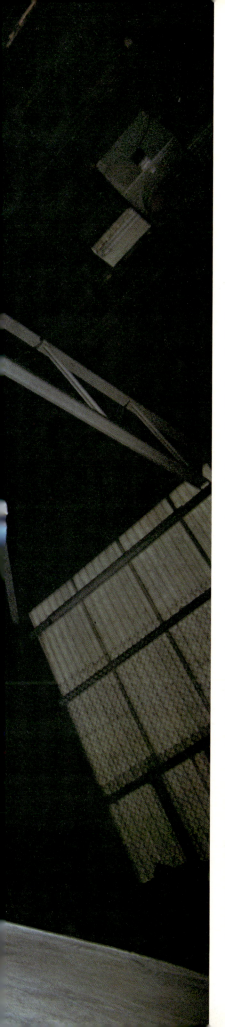

Rampstall

Hit the ramp at medium speed and start to pull up on the front as you climb. Because the idea of this stunt is to get the back wheel as close to the end of the ramp as possible, you have to keep a close eye on the edge of the ramp and be ready to apply the brake. By the time the rear wheel gets to the edge you should be up and in the wheelie position. Now you must flex your body, ready for pulling the bike up into the air. Because you're already on the edge of catastrophe when you lift the bike, you also want to move it backwards in the air. The idea is to land both wheels at the same time, so you have get the same angle as the ramp. Once you've landed, finish with a rollback.

180 pivot/spin

Approach the ramp at medium speed, off the seat. As you climb the ramp lift the front, apply the rear brake, pull the bike close in to your body and spin, putting the front down when you have twisted 180°.

540 pivot/spin

Approach the ramp at medium speed. As you climb the ramp tense your body for what is one hell of a spin, apply the rear brake, lift the front end and pull the bike in to your body, and force the bike round using your arms. Unless you have the bike high and in to your body you will not get round for the full 540°.

A pivot on the back wheel.

How to build your own small ramp

What you need:
6 pieces of planed timber
   3.3m × 70mm × 45mm
2 pieces of planed timber
   2.4m × 70mm × 45mm
1 sheet of 15mm exterior
   plywood, 1220 × 2440mm
1 piece of 12mm exterior
   plywood, 1220 × 2000mm
$\frac{1}{2}$ kilo of $1\frac{1}{2}$″, and $\frac{1}{2}$ kilo of 2″
   galvanized nails
8 × 4″ nails
saw, hammer, measuring tape, sandpaper, protractor, 30° and 60° geometry square

Instructions
1 Cut the shapes A–D from the planed timber
2 Cut shapes F and G from 12mm ply
3 Construct 3 trusses as shown in fig. b by nailing the plywood plates to the timber with $1\frac{1}{2}$″ nails. Use about 20 nails for each plate
4 Fix the cross-members E with plywood plates and use the 4″ nails to construct the frame as shown in fig. a
5 Cut the 15mm plywood sheet into two pieces as shown in fig. b
6 Fix the larger piece of plywood to the upper ramp using 2″ nails at 100mm intervals into truses and cross-members
7 Fix the small piece of ply in the same way
8 Sandpaper edges of ply.

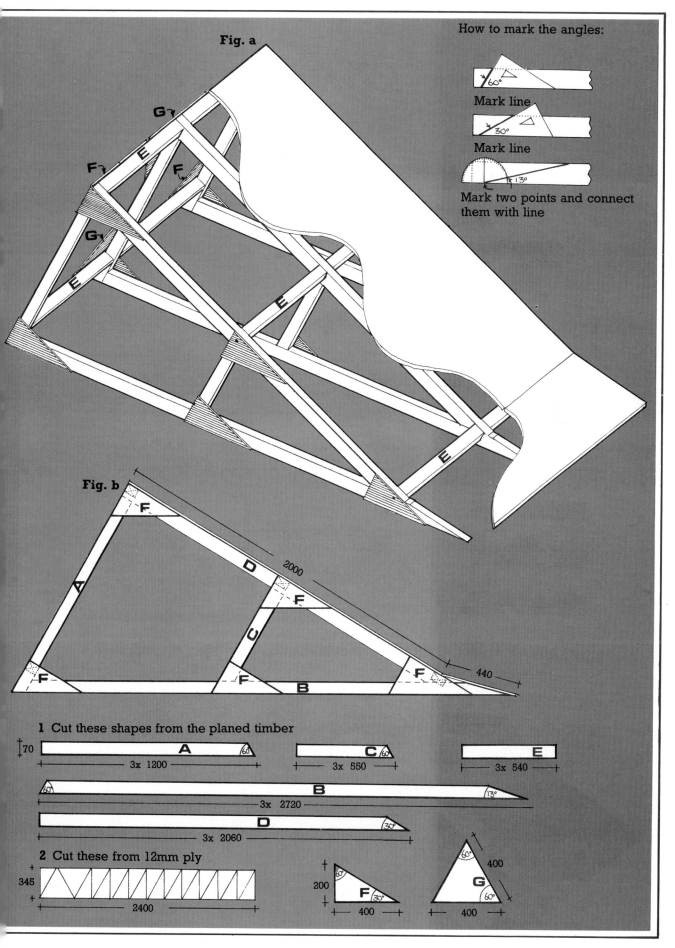

How to mark the angles:

Mark line

Mark line

Mark two points and connect them with line

Fig. a

Fig. b

1 Cut these shapes from the planed timber

2 Cut these from 12mm ply

37

Large Ramp

Once you're working on the large ramp then all the experience you have gained on the ground and on the small ramp will prove invaluable. The feel you have built up for judging the end of the ramp and the awareness of where the sides are become crucial when, instead of riding up a slope of a metre or so, you are climbing higher than two metres.

As for the small ramp, it is important to get the feel of the new shape and dimensions by practising the easier tricks first. Get to gauge the correct speed for reaching the top of the ramp, and being able to handle the momentum that the large ramp gives is also important, especially for riding out and rolling back.

First of all just get used to riding up the ramp, getting closer and closer to the top with your front wheel. Every time you do this you are getting good practice at rolling back. The next step is to take the front wheel further than the ledge, controlling the bars so you don't pitch forward. This is the first stage of a kickturn and a rampstall, without the real risk that the actual trick entails.

After several goes at this it is time to try a straightforward 180 pivot from halfway up the ramp. Just ride in at medium pace and when you feel happy, pull the rear brake on, flex your body ready for the twist and pivot the bike 180°. Bring the front wheel down and ride out. What you have just done is in fact a kickturn but you have done it further down the ramp than is generally expected. Now, after as much practice as you feel you need to boost your confidence, it is time to go for broke – your first kickturn on the large ramp!

Up up and away and it's a quarter-pipe launch.

Kickturn

Make a medium speed approach. You know the ramp by now and you know what sort of pace you need to get to the top. For a good kickturn you need to get the back wheel to the top of the ramp. As you get close to the ledge start pulling on the bars and keep the line of your body over the seat as you extend your body from the flexed position. Once you hit the top pull the bike in to your body, apply the back brake and flip the bike round. Pivot to 180°, push down on the bars and ride out.

One-foot kickturn

Same as for the basic large ramp kickturn but things change when you get to the top. Once you've pulled the bike in to your body and applied the brake you are into the turn, and this is the time to extend the leg for a straight kick. Having achieved the extended leg position you now let the front end down and bring the foot back to the pedal.

One-hand one-foot kickturn

Same as for the previous stunt but as the leg is extended so, at the same time, is the arm on the same side as the extended foot.

Fakie air

Speed and the shape of the ramp will take you through this one, as long as you stay cool, and keep the bike straight.

Make for the ramp at medium to fast speed, standing, with your body straight up from the cranks. When the front wheel has passed the ledge and the cranks are level with it you need to start going back the way you came. By now, if you have judged it right, this should happen naturally. Ideally, both wheels want to land together and you just roll back to complete the stunt.

Right: Dropping back in off the quarter-pipe platform.

Pop-out

You need to feel pretty confident that you've mastered the large ramp before you have a go at this one, because if it goes wrong you are into freefall!

Get to the ramp at slightly more than medium speed but not flat out. Roll up the ramp standing, let the bike run out of steam and get your weight forward over the bars. When you reach the top use your arms to pull the bike upwards. When the back wheel is just below the ledge start to turn (you choose whichever direction you feel comfortable going). You're still pulling upwards because you have to get the back wheel to land on the platform. Just before touchdown put the rear brake on and get the appropriate foot off the pedal, ready to stand with one foot on the platform and one on the pedal and the front held high.

Drop-in

Once you've 'popped-out' there aren't many other ways of reaching terra-firma than using the drop-in! The end of the pop-out is the beginning of the drop-in.

Stand with one foot on the pedal and the other on the ramp platform with the rear brake on. The front is high, grips held firm. Let the front drop, keep the brake on and as the front wheel drops just below the ledge get the standing foot back on the pedal. At this point the weight should be over the seat. As the bike falls close to the ramp let the brake off and push down on the front and ride out.

The critical moments of an aerial, coming down to a stylish landing on the quarter-pipe.

40

One-hand one-foot drop-in

Having mastered the basic drop-in you should, with a bit of practice, manage this one. Your problems begin when you have to let go of the bars. With one foot on the pedal and one on the platform, pull the bike high by the bars. With the coaster or the handbrake on firmly, balance on the pedal, extend the spare arm fully in the air and kick the leg that was on the platform out straight and as high into the air as you can. While you are doing all this you have to keep the bars straight with the one hand and start the drop-in. Once the front wheel is just below the ledge of the ramp it's time to get your bits and pieces back to the bike, so with the ramp coming up fast, both hands on the bars and both feet on the pedals you bring the front wheel down and ride out.

Aerial

Ride into the ramp fast though not flat out. Flex your knees and body as you climb. Let the bike climb and follow the shape of the ramp, because you want to make contact after the turn with the first third of the pipe. Once you get height above the ramp pull the bike in and begin the turn, which starts from the bars. By the time you've reached maximum height you should be half way round. As you complete the turn force the front down, make your landing and ride out.

Reverse rockwalk off a large ramp

Roll back from the top of the ramp, standing and at medium speed. Don't roll back too far; you need to get the first pivot in early. With your weight to the back, lift on the bars and bring the front end round 180°. As soon as the front wheel is down shift yourself to the front of the bike and bring the back round to complete another 180°. On touchdown shift your weight back to the rear, pull the front up and start pedalling as you bring it round for the final 180° before riding out.

41

540 rollback

This one starts with a quite fast rollback off the large ramp. Get over the back and put the rear brake on, but not too hard. Start to turn the wheel into your turn. Pull up on the bars as you feel the spin, then pull the bars even further in to your body. Now the bike should be high and as close to your body as you can get it. You have done your first bit – the 360°; now comes the crucial part. Using your body you have to keep spinning, still holding the bike in to your body and keeping it high and still keeping the brake on. When you have got round the other 180°, set the front wheel down and ride out.

Fun stuff

These are the tricks you won't actually be asked to do in a competition, nor will you find them in any freestyle manual, but they are to be seen when a group of freestylers get together and want to have fun.

Lay-back glide

You need stunt-nuts for this one. Ride at medium pace on a flat surface. Holding the bars with one hand, transfer your first foot to the stunt-nuts at the back, on the opposite side of the bike. If you have led with your right foot then you now have your left foot on the pedal and your right on the same side of the bike but on the rear stunt-nut.

Now transfer your left foot from the pedal to the front stunt-nut. You are now standing feet fully astride from front to back. Just to make it look good you can let go of the bars and take up a star position as you glide along, but that isn't the trick.

Next you start to bend at the knees and get your backside down low. To balance this movement to one side you need to let the bike out in the opposite direction. In this way you get the bike as horizontally close to the ground as you can.

Coming in to land after a successful mission in space!

Above: Remembering the pipe's atmosphere.

Left: Flattening out from the Bowl quarter-pipe.

Crab ride (from a bar-hop)

Perform the bar-hop as shown on page 28. Once you're over the front get your feet onto the stunt-nuts while you get your balance. With your hands stretched out behind, keep a good grip of the bars and then shift your feet back to the pedals. You may have to fumble a bit but you will soon find them. Now in this very awkward position you pedal your bike round. To finish, if you want a bit of the flash stuff, you can reverse the process going back over the bars.

43

Two's up

This is good if you can stop laughing. This bit of fun is performed by two riders with only one bike. Each rider takes up a position on the pedal on his side of the bike with his outside foot on the pedal and the free one trailing back. The rider with the high pedal pushes down and the other rider should be brought upwards by the momentum of crank, though he will assist by taking the weight off his pedal by supporting himself with his arms. As one rider pushes down on the pedal and the other rider rises to the top of the crank so the opposite rider starts the downward momentum. In this way both riders are moving rather in the way that a crankshaft in an engine does when it turns.

Horizontal mobile press-up

You need a lot of strength in your arms and thighs for this one, because you will be doing a virtual press-up without having your feet on the ground. Coast at medium pace with a good clear run in front of you. When you have balance lean forward, place one hand at the base of the head-set downpipe and the other on the junction with the crossbar and the fork housing. Take a good grip and lift your back end and legs off the bike and get them out straight and just above the seat. Hold the horizontal position as long as you can.

Buckin' bronco

This one really is a mixture of endos and pogos. The endos are initiated by using the front brake and they turn into front wheel pogos when you start bouncing on the front wheel. Do a few bounces on the front wheel until you feel you are losing it, then pull back over the seat, pull the bars up and go into the pogo routine. After a few bounces on the back wheel dive back into the endo and then into the front wheel pogos. The buckin' bronco is shown in the step-by-step sequence on page 24.

How to build a large ramp

What you need:
7 pieces of planed timber
    1.8m × 70mm × 45mm
4 pieces 2.1m × 70mm × 45mm
6 pieces 2.4m × 70mm × 45mm
2 sheets of 6.5mm exterior
    plywood, 1525 × 3050mm
1 sheet of 15mm exterior
    plywood, 1525 × 600mm
1 sheet of 12mm exterior
    plywood, 865 × 2000mm
½ kilo of 1½" and ½ kilo 2"
    galvanized nails
16 × 4" nails
the same tools as for the small ramp

Instructions

1 Cut shapes H–P from the planed timber
2 Cut shapes R and S from 12mm ply
3 Construct 3 trusses as shown in fig. b by nailing the plywood plates to the timber with 1½" nails. Use about 20 nails for each plate
4 Fix the cross-members N and P with plywood plates and use the 4" nails to construct the frame as shown in fig. a
5 Fix the 15mm sheet of plywood to the top of the ramp, using 2" nails at 100mm intervals into trusses and cross-members

6 Fix the top edge of one sheet of 6.5mm plywood to the upper ramp, using 1½" nails at 200mm intervals into the cross-members, taking care to bring the edge flush with the upper face of the ledge. Push the ramp ply back into a curve and fix it to the cross-members P with 2" nails at 200mm intervals, working down from the top
7 Fix the second sheet of 6.5mm ply over the first with 2" nails placed at 200mm intervals into the cross-members. Work down from the top and push the sheet of ply down into contact with the lower sheet
8 Sandpaper edges of ply.

1 Cut these shapes from the planed timber

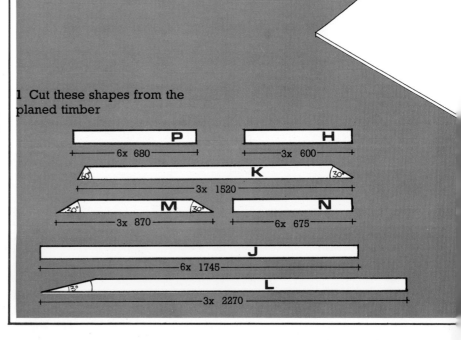

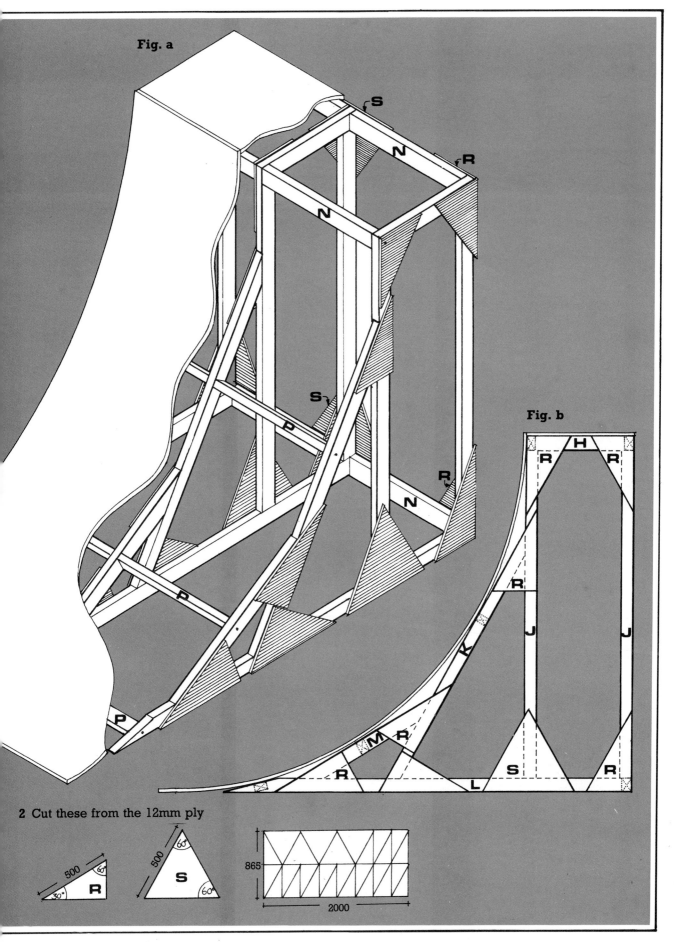

Fig. a

S

N

R

N

S

P

S

R

Fig. b

H

R R

R

J J

K

R

M R

R L S R

P

P

P

2 Cut these from the 12mm ply

500 60°

30° 60° 60° 500 60°

R **S**

865

2000

The wall-of-death – it's a long way down!

Right: A table-top out of the Clover Leaf.

The Bowl

When Thomas Tusser said some five hundred years ago that 'it was an ill wind that blew nobody any good' it is certain that he wasn't thinking of the skateboard phenomenon, yet his words are ideally suited to what has taken place in the last few years.

Skateboarding arrived in this country from across the Atlantic with a massive explosion. Crazes come and go but this one, the pundits said, was here to stay. All the signs were that they were right. Unfortunately, as we now know, they were wrong. As quickly as it electrified the imagination of the country's youngsters, so it faded from the scene. For those who had invested in it heavily it was indeed an ill wind, yet it did blow somebody some good. And that 'somebody' is the BMX fraternity. The skate bowl, with its beautifully contoured ups and downs, its sweeping bowls and sculptured walls is ideal for the BMX freestyler, and it is in the spectacular environment of the 'Bowls' that some of the best freestyling can be seen. The 'Bowl' offers an area for everyone from the novice to the expert in which to learn or to show just how good he is.

The Performance Bowl is perhaps the place where you will find the novice tentatively feeling his way about the world of 'Bowl' freestyling. It is here he can ride on the beautifully smooth concrete finish and use the graded sides as ramps. Most ground-work competitions take place in this area and it is here that you will see things like slaloms, bunny-hops, wheelies and pogos taking place.

The short ramps are ideal for beginners to start experimenting with things like kickturns, 180s and ramp endos without the uncertainty of having a narrow ramp where you can go off the sides. It is also ideal for making a start on rollbacks and, of course, sliders, where the really smooth surface is great.

The Performance Bowl is ideal for putting together routines where one manoeuvre can lead smoothly into another, especially when the graded sides are used. Combinations like a front-wheel endo into a rollback, a 180 turn and finishing with a coaster wheelie are examples of the sort of work an average freestyler might like to put together in the Performance Bowl.

For a mixture of sheer speed and excitement, the Tunnel takes a lot of beating. This is a long shaft where the rider can start downhill to get his speed up, and gradually climbs to a very sudden, almost sheer, rise which will take him out of the Tunnel onto flat ground. When you are anywhere near the Tunnel as a spectator keep your eyes open for the sudden shock of riders coming from nowhere and soaring through the sky. The Tunnel is there for riders to leap out of. That is its design and a steady stream of riders coming down the Tunnel ensures that only the stupid are going to try aerials in it.

Right: The Tunnel

Top right: The Snake Pit

Far right: The Clover Leaf

The idea at the end of the Tunnel is to have enough speed to get some air when you start flying. Without enough speed there is always the chance that you won't clear the lip and will roll back down in the direction you just came from; that isn't so funny if other riders happen to be coming up behind.

The important thing with the Tunnel is that you don't go in there until you are confident that you can handle this sort of action. You can get some idea of your ability to get out of the Tunnel by practising in the Performance Bowl on the graded ramps. These are easier and less sheer but they will tell you something about how fast you need to go and the sort of control you need to have in the Tunnel.

Right: Time to go home!

Opposite: Table-topping out of the Clover.

Below: Kickturn par excellence on the ridge of the Performance Bowl.

51

When you can get height from the Tunnel then you have to start thinking seriously about your landings. Even if you have the bike for the job you won't do it a lot of good if you land from about two metres in the air with a gigantic thud. Practise from the start putting your bike down softly. The way to do this is to pull the bike up to your body as you hit the highest point of your jump, then just before you land extend it to the ground and telescope yourself back to it on touchdown. It acts as a shock absorber in cushioning the impact and it looks a lot better.

All sorts of things happen when riders come out of the Tunnel, not all of them intended. It will help a lot if you know before setting off exactly what you are going to do when ejection time comes. Another important thing is to check before you go in that whatever trick you want to do is feasible in the area available for landing.

The most common stunt out of the Tunnel is a straightforward jump and a good landing. The more ambitious however will be doing 360° turns before touching down, while others will come out doing a little number known as the parachute jump. This is where the rider exits with the bike ahead of him and he is hanging back from the bars. Often when the rider realises that all is not well for a straightforward jump because he has too much speed or too much height, or both he will convert to the Parachute as a way of getting out with dignity and not over-shooting the landing space.

Left: Humps and bumps – good fun and good practice.

Top right: A slalom taking place in the Performance Bowl.

Right: A wheelie in the competition.

Far right: A bunny-hop competition for junior riders.

The next area of supreme excitement is the 'Clover Leaf'. This is a very deep bowl with four segments shaped like a clover leaf. The name of the game when you get down there is to use the walls and contours to put together a swinging routine of aerials, jumps and kickturns as you swoop from one leaf to another. The tips of each leaf are not very far apart, so after diving back into the bowl from one aerial you are pretty soon climbing the wall on the other side and getting ready for another dynamic take-off on the other side. The Clover Leaf is superb for doing pop-outs and drop-ins. Where two riders or more are sufficiently confident it is a great area for putting together some breathtaking formation work, but don't attempt it unless you really have the timing bit down to perfection. Some skateparks have runways leading down to the 'Clover' which means it can be used for the most hair-raising leaps into space at fantastic speeds.

Right: Getting it straight on the ridge.

Far right: Endo on the stunt-nuts.

Below: Flat and going for broke.

Most Bowls also have an undulating 'Fun Area' where riders can just ride around over the humps and bumps and experiment.

Another small chute which is deep and has high sides for getting the aerials perfected can usually be found in most Bowls. The walls of this small chute are also good for trying the 'wall-of-death' rides.

The 'Main Bowl' is perhaps the most exciting area in the Bowl and the place where the really brave get totally airborne. It is usually about five metres deep with a twelve-metre run down into the deepest point where a steep climb takes the rider towards the clouds. Most competitions for aerials, pop-outs and drop-ins take place in the Main Bowl. The wall-of-death can be performed at extraordinary speeds there.

Right: The Performance Bowl with graded sides.

Far right: After running up the graded side the rider can roll back, pivot slide or go into hop-backs.

Below: The freestyler's answer to jams.

Freestyle Competition

Racing may be the foremost aspect of BMX but the freestyle competition takes a great deal of beating when it comes to the spectacular. Death-defying aerials, 360° and even 540° turns in mid-air, and the most incredible leaps over anything from a row of bodies to a lengthwise saloon car are all part of the sizzling competition which is never short of a good crowd and strong vocal appreciation.

Freestyle competitions are staged on two different structures, the skateboard park and the ramp competition. Within these two, similar stunts are judged but of course they are performed on different surfaces. To find out when there are competitions on near you, check out the BMX press regularly.

Drop-in off a quarter-pipe platform.

Whether the competition is held using ramps or the skateboards there is usually a groundwork section to set the show in motion. This can consist of a series of compulsory exercises which the rider will have to perform in a given time. A typical set of tasks may include a bunny-hop, a slalom round rigidly spaced obstacles, a measured wheelie, a pogo, an endo, a rollback, a 180 kickturn, a 360 turn, and a rockwalk.

Within these compulsory exercises the rider will be allowed to link his display with his own expressions of freestyling, and may raise the pace a little with some rollback sliders, one-hand or one-foot endos and those crowd-pleasing frame-stands.

So what are the judges looking for when the rider performs his routine? They will be looking for the smooth way in which the rider goes through his

Bunny-hopping a bike.

programme, moving from one exercise to another. They will be marking on style and artistic impression. Some competitions give marks for what a rider achieves with each aspect of the marking system, while others give a rider a certain number of points at the outset of his programme and make deductions to reflect his level of performance. Apart from winning points for the categories mentioned the rider will lose points for falling, putting a foot down, knocking down obstacles, going outside permitted areas or not completing a move.

Competitions are organised in age groups, getting more difficult as the riders' age increases. Certain skills are made more difficult by reducing the space in which a rider can manoeuvre, or, in the case of a bunny-hop, the bar is raised to suit the age group. Slaloms are made more difficult by closing the space between obstacles. All groups of exercises have a certain time for completion.

Most competitions allow the rider to mix his own voluntary scheme and a certain time is usually allocated for completing these. Conditions are sometimes imposed to forbid the repetition of any stunt in the programme. In the voluntary class the judges will look for originality in the way the programme is put together, and the degree of difficulty will also affect marks.

When the competition is held in a skatebowl, compulsory exercises are judged in the Clover Bowl and also in the Performance Bowl. A typical Clover-Bowl programme might include an aerial, drop-in, pivots and pop-outs, while the Performance-Bowl programme might include a straight elevator (drop-in), a pop-out of the Main Bowl, different types of aerials and a wall-of-death entry.

Where ramps are being used, a similar programme is found, except of course exercises like the wall-of-death entry which can only be performed in an area like the Performance Bowl. Exercises like drop-ins and pop-outs can be performed on the large ramp if it has a built-in platform at the top. Good luck, and enjoy yourself.

How to walk round your bike while it's moving!

Bottom left: Flat as a pancake.

Bottom: Dropping in and really on the lip.

Below: Drop-ins have to be stylish. The nearer the wheel to the rim, the better.